D0535846

# What to Do When Your Family Is in Debt

Rachel Lynette

**PowerKiDS** press

New York

Published in 2010 by The Rosen Publishing Group, Inc.
29 East 21st Street, New York, NY 10010

First Edition

Editor: Joanne Randolph
Book Design: Julio Gil
Photo Researcher: Jessica Gerweck

Photo Credits: Cover Flynn Larsen/Getty Images; pp. 4, 8, 14, 16, 20 Shutterstock.com; p. 6 © Stuart Pearce/age fotostock; p. 10 Emmanuel Faure/Getty Images; p. 12 Betsie Van der Meer/Getty Images; p. 18 David Harry Stewart/Getty Images.

Library of Congress Cataloging-in-Publication Data

Lynette, Rachel.
  What to do when your family is in debt / Rachel Lynette. — 1st ed.
    p. cm. — (Let's work it out)
  Includes index.
  ISBN 978-1-4358-9341-2 (library binding) — ISBN 978-1-4358-9770-0 (pbk.) —
ISBN 978-1-4358-9771-7 (6-pack)
  1. Debt—Juvenile literature. 2. Consumer credit—Juvenile literature. I. Title.
  HG3755.L96 2010
  332.024'02—dc22
                                        2009027405

Manufactured in the United States of America

CPSIA Compliance Information: Batch #WW10PK: For Further Information contact Rosen Publishing, New York, New York at 1-800-237-9932

# Contents

*Most people need to take out a loan, or borrow money, to buy a car. Taking out a loan means you are now in debt.*

# What Is Debt?

Have you ever wanted something, but you did not have enough money to pay for it? When adults want something that they do not have enough money for, such as a new car or a boat, they sometimes borrow the money. When people borrow money, they must pay it back with **interest**. Interest is money that must be paid in addition to the amount that was borrowed.

If a family borrows too much money, they may not be able to pay it back. The longer a family takes to pay back a debt, the more interest they will have to pay. Once a family borrows money, they are in debt.

Credit cards are an easy way to pay for goods. Credit cards also make it easy for people to spend more than they have.

# How Did We Get Here?

When people borrow money, they generally pay it back in payments that they make once a month. People often borrow money for a house or a car. Sometimes people agree to payments that are too high for them.

Many people get into debt by using **credit cards**. Using a credit card is a way to borrow money. It is easy to use a credit card. Sometimes people buy a lot of things using their credit cards but do not think about how they will pay for them. Credit cards often have high interest rates. Some people use several different credit cards. Then they end up with even more money to pay back!

*We need healthy food, but sometimes people pick costly food or they buy too much. These things can put your family in debt.*

# Needs and Wants

There are things that you need and things that you want. You need food, clothing, and a place to live. It is important that you and your family always get what you need. You may want things like a new toy or an **expensive** pair of shoes. You do not need these things to live, though.

Often, families get into debt by buying too many of the things they want. Your family may be able to get out of debt by buying only what you need. It can be hard not to get things that you want, but it is more important that you have enough money to pay for the things you need.

*Talk to your family about the things you value most. If you still want to take karate classes, what can you give up to make the family budget work?*

# What Is the Plan?

If your family is in debt, your parents will need to take a closer look at how they spend their money. One thing that can help is to make a family **budget**. A budget shows everything your family spends money on and how much money is needed for each thing. Is there anything you can give up, such as going to the movies, to help cut back on family spending?

When a family agrees to stick to their budget, they do not spend money on things that are not on it. A budget can help keep spending under control. Sticking to a budget is not always easy, but it is a great way to get out of debt! You can help by not asking for things that are not in the budget.

*Helping your mom out in the kitchen will make her feel less stressed and tired. A few hugs will help her, too!*

# Ways to Help

Sometimes the best way to get out of debt is to make more money. Your parent may work longer hours or even take a second job to get out of debt. You may not get to spend much time with your parent while she is working to get out of debt. You may have to spend more time with a sitter or at day care.

When your parent is at home, she may feel **stressed** and tired. You can make things better by finding ways to help around the house. Can you fold the clothes or do the dishes? Helping out is a great way to make things less stressful!

If your family is in debt, you may feel like you are giving up a lot. Cutting back will help your family in the long run, though.

# Debt and Me

What does your family being in debt have to do with you? A lot! When a family is working to pay back its debt, it has an effect on everyone in the family. Just like your parents, you may have to give up some of the things you want. You may not get new toys or clothes. You may not get to do some of the things you enjoy, such as going to the movies or taking dance classes.

You may also feel like there is more stress in your house. Your parents may be worried about rising interest rates or making **mortgage** payments. Banks and credit card companies may be calling your home to ask about missing payments.

Doing fun things outdoors, such as flying a kite, does not cost money. Not only that, but they will make everyone feel better!

# Do Things Together

What can you do when your parents are stressed because of their debt? First, remember that debt is a grown-up problem. There are things you can do to help your parents, but it is not your job to get your family out of debt. You can help your parents deal with stress by coming up with fun, free things you can do as a family, such as taking a bike ride or having a picnic together.

It can help to remember that if your family sticks to their budget and follows a plan, you will not always be in debt. Someday, your family's debts will be paid off. When your family pays off its debts, things will not be so stressful.

*Debt can be a hard idea to understand. Talking to your parents will help you make sense of what is happening.*

# Talk About It

One of the best ways to deal with stress is to talk about it. If you are feeling worried or scared about your family's debt, talk to your parents about it. Talking about your feelings can help you feel better. Your parents may also be able to help you understand how your family is getting out of debt.

It may also help to talk to an adult outside your family. Is there an adult that you like and trust? You may be able to talk to a teacher, coach, or a **counselor** at school. Even talking to a friend will help you feel better. You do not have to keep your feelings inside.

*Instead of paying for a babysitter, your parents might ask your grandparents to watch you more often.*

# Asking for Help

If your family is in debt, your parents may ask for help. Often, people ask their families to help. Your grandparents or aunts and uncles may be able to help. They may be able to help with food or pay some of the bills. They may be able to take care of you while your parents work.

Sometimes, people get help from the state or from a **charity**. Your family may go on **welfare** for a while. You do not need to feel **ashamed** if your family is getting help. You are doing what you need to do to pay off your debts. Remember, everyone needs help sometimes!

# Learn and Grow

Being in debt has likely taught you a lot about yourself and your family. You may have learned that your family can depend on you to help. You may have learned that you do not need to buy new things to be happy. You may be feeling proud of yourself and your parents. Getting out of debt is a big **accomplishment**!

You are also learning a lot for the future. Someday, you will be an adult. You will decide how to spend your own money. What have you learned about getting into debt? What can you do to make sure that you stay out of debt?

# Glossary

accomplishment (uh-KOM-plish-ment)  Something a person finishes well.

ashamed (uh-SHAYMD)  Uncomfortable because of something you did.

budget (BUH-jit)  A plan to spend a certain amount of money in a period of time.

charity (CHER-uh-tee)  A group that gives help to the needy.

counselor (KOWN-seh-ler)  Someone who talks with people about their feelings and problems and who gives advice.

credit cards (KREH-dit KAHRDZ)  Cards used to buy something with an agreement to pay for it later.

expensive (ik-SPENT-siv)  Costing a lot of money.

interest (IN-ter-est)  The extra cost that someone pays in order to borrow money.

mortgage (MAWR-gij)  An agreement to use a building or a piece of land as security for a loan. If the loan is not paid back, the lender gets to keep the building or land.

stressed (STREST)  Worried or feeling bad because of a problem.

welfare (WEL-fehr)  Programs that give help to poor people.

# Index

# Web Sites

Due to the changing nature of Internet links, PowerKids Press has developed an online list of Web sites related to the subject of this book. This site is updated regularly. Please use this link to access the list:

www.powerkidslinks.com/lwio/debt/